HERE ALONG CAZENOVIA CREEK

Here Along Cazenovia Creek

Ruth Thompson

Saddle Road Press

Here Along Cazenovia Creek
(Revised Edition)
© 2011, 2017 by Ruth Thompson

Saddle Road Press
Hilo, Hawai'i
www.saddleroadpress.com

www.ruththompson.net

All rights reserved. No part of this book may be reproduced or transmitted in any form or by any means without written permission of the author.

Book design by Don Mitchell
Cover illustration by Don Mitchell
Author photograph by Tania Pryputniewicz

ISBN 978-0-9833072-0-4

For Don

Table of Contents

Preface to the Revised Edition	9
Spring by Cazenovia Creek	11
Midsummer	16
The Lake	20
Fat Time	22
Kaffir Lily	24
After the Storm	25
All Saints Eve	26
November by Cazenovia Creek	27
First Snow	28
Winter Solstice	29
Winter in Buffalo	30
Acknowledgments	32
About Ruth Thompson	33

Preface to the Revised Edition

Until I moved east from California to an old farmhouse set on the banks of Cazenovia Creek in Colden, New York, I had never lived in a place with four distinct seasons.

I arrived when the leaves were beginning to turn — and fell into the madness of love. I wandered in the woods, cramming my pockets with their banked fires. I stared at the intense blue of the sky. I wrote a love poem, "Fat Time." And then, as the year turned, I wrote other love poems to other seasons, to an astonishing and deeply satisfying landscape of sensory transformation.

I had never known what the winter solstice meant until I lived along Cazenovia Creek. I had never burrowed deep, never wakened to utter white silence. I had never knelt to worship a fragile bulb pushing through mud-gray ice after long darkness. I had never struggled to move through August air heavy with the respiration of swollen leaves, never watched young deer play leapfrog in the meadow on long midsummer evenings.

Those love poems to the hill country of western New York became this book, *Here Along Cazenovia Creek*, which changed my life in more ways than I can count. I discovered that other people did want to read praise poems— did adore, as I did, the astonishing fierce joy of spring. And when the book was choreographed and performed as "The Seasons" with the celebrated Japanese dancer Shizuno Nasu, another door opened— to collaboration between movement and words.

   I still love these poems, and I still love the house along Cazenovia Creek, though I no longer live there and it has changed. In honor of that place and all it meant to me, I offer this new edition of *Here Along Cazenovia Creek*, with Don Mitchell's beautiful cover photograph of the trees across the Creek— the same ones I fell in love with many years ago.

Ruth Thompson
January, 2017

Spring by Cazenovia Creek

i

The roses have come through
though some are dead to the ankles.

Now, in this cheerful air
they must be feeling pain
where the dead places are stretched
by little flames of juice—

when it catches they burn
burgundy and green and green.

ii

Greek Persephone
in her dry meadows
could linger, could fritter
picking orchids and anemones

but here
earth turns faster
we are all in a hurry—
the hooves, the wheels
are upon you—

breed! breed!
before the dark.

iii

One morning the sky is full of noise
and here they come, yonking
along the creek, circling down, skidding
in the icy sedge, checking it out,
settling in.

A few stragglers—
Hey, you got any room down there?
No! Get lost!—

and suddenly
it's a neighborhood.

iv

Everywhere up and down the road—
yelling their wares beside mailboxes,
along driveways and porches—

forsythia and Schiaparelli-colored quinces—
and tulips and daffodils, yellow and orange and purple
and scarlet poppies the size of sunflowers
their ripe black hearts already spilling seed

and chartreuse maple leaves untwirling
over the dark mud and slick gray sheen of ice.

The whole world is trumpets bellowing
as loudly as they can,
and not in any tune but their own

none of it composed or assonant
or orchestrated or seemly—
everything just roostering out

because they cannot wait!
they have to ring the bells and shout
Yes! Yes!

v

The green dog runs beside me
following his pleasure,
circling back from time to time

from rocky places or it may be
doorways

and he is green because
new grass is springing,
fine and thick
through the old guard hairs

on his back, which is redolent
of sun and dust and bitter herbs

and he says
Smell Here Now.

vi

It's like you turn your head
for a moment or close your eyes

for a moment, like the pig-iron-
colored frost still has it all locked
for a moment longer and then

faster than you can catch in your wide
palms, in your wide eyes—

saffron-veined crocuses pushing through the ice,
then clouds of crabapples and willows and mauve
rhododendrons
and the cherry tree pouring down snow
into pools of grape hyacinths and forget-me-nots

and lilies of the valley, smelling
like that dream you had about the angel,

and purple irises and lilacs in clusters
of scented grapes, and wisteria—
and suddenly every roadside white and purple
with daisies and wild phlox

and then all along the fence,
fat mops of peonies, as big as your head,
and Renoir-fleshed roses, all
pink shoulders and gold ribbons,
and the lilies already two feet high—

and you are spinning around
to catch it inside your eyes before—

but it won't stop,
it is galloping downhill, days
like catherine wheels—

everything roistering, everything
busy being what it exactly
is, just as fatly and deliciously
as possible— like little pigs grunting
and sucking it up through their feet,
mouths open to the rain, to the held hose

and you would cry Wait!
but you're already twelve miles
down the road
and suddenly it's

vii

Fig-ripe, falling open,
heavy-breasted, deliquescing.

Melon sky, lightning-split
spitting seeds of thunder.

Caught in the grasses,
light, light, light!

Sugar shimmering in the veins.
On the skin, a slick of sweet.

Midsummer

i

One day the earth is flat.

The next, it is fat with leaves.

On the third, it pours forth bodies.

ii

Morning sun butters the siding.

Light sharp as a new green shoot
strikes through the open door.

Outside, the world is made of grass,
impossible and delicious as a painting.

iii

Noon seeps upward
from small muddy feet of grasses

fills the garden with smoky golden waters
where white butterflies swim in flocks like fish.

iv

At the feeder the chickadees
peck through, discard,
picky as women squeezing fruit.

Chipmunks rescue dropped seeds, scramble
to store them in my winter shoes.

v

The wasps are at the sugar water
again, driving off the hummingbirds

and the robin is distraught, babies loose,
a thousand dangers.

vi

Throughout the long dusk
two fawns leap-
frog in the meadow.

vii

The maples darken, descend.

Moisture gathers in corners.
The sofa steams gently.

Damp emerges through the seats of pants
paperbacks curl from the tables

a foot's imprint on the rug
fills slowly with a film of water

viii

Thunder splits the cracked skull of sky:
Inside, nothing but light!

ix

We are very pregnant.
We walk with effort.
Why move?

We can feel it in our thighs and buttocks:
the downward pull, the weight.
An old sun's gravity.

x

Lying in the sun, we remember
how we poured forth
pheromones, how we cast
our beauty into the bright air of chance.

xi

The garden sits
like a woman
with too many children.

Flower heads fold, topple
under their own weight.

In the woods,
a falling off.

xii

One morning:
frost, raking light, sharp
shapes of leaves, shadow
of hanging hose.

xiii

A shiver in the neck. The hairs rise.
It is not emptied yet, but soon.

xiv

Purple asters, big-headed and little-
headed, blue stars and white stars
and tiny blue and white clouds

and the tiger colors of the maple leaves.

xv

This morning they are calling
to one another from the pine tree.
Five repeated calls. And answers
from far away.

The Lake

In this sky-cloud surface,
trees reflect the world of trees.
They root in lake-root,
branches cup and drink.

Lake is in tree, tree
is in lake. Deep below,
water again, caverns-full—
lake secretly repeats itself.

Above, the world of cloud—
more and more light,
less and less cloud:
the lake of the sky.

Between, this lucent
membrane, belled
between elements, floats
over clear water, pale

brown water, muddy
water, sludge. They say
somewhere below it ends:
everything we see is seepage.

Dead leaves like motes of sun
return to earth through golden
water. Their light bubbles
upward, dissolves in sky.

Lake itself rises, becomes
cloud, falls again in rain. Wind
rustles water, leaves rustle
air. Murmur of thunder,

murmur of rain, slap
of water on piers, of boat
on water, thud of wing-beat,
of paddle-steamer,

plash of oars, gull-cry,
voices over water calling.

Fat Time

Under purest ultramarine the raised
goblets of trees overrun with gold.
We should be reeling drunk and portly as groundhogs
through these windfalls of russet, citron, bronze,
chartreuse.

Everywhere color pools like butter, like oil of ripe nuts,
like piles of oranges under a striped tent.

Oh, let us be greedy of eyeball,
pigs scuffling in this gorgeous swill!
Let us cud this day
and spend the winter ruminant.

Let us write fat poems, and be careless.
Let us go bumbling about in wonder, legs
coated with goldenrod and smelling of acorns.

Let us be unctuous with scarlet and marigold,
larder them here, behind our foreheads
to glow in the brain's lamps
in the time of need.

Each tree a sun!
Let us stare, let us be sunstruck!
Let us throw away caution,
emblazon our retinas
with the flare and flame of it

so that in the unleavened winter
this vermilion spill, this skyfall,
these oils of tangerine, smears of ochre and maroon
will heat a spare poem, dazzle the eye's window,
feed us like holy deer on the blank canvas of snow.

KAFFIR LILY

Outside the kitchen window
red fuses fire, flare into webs
of crimson, and are taken
by the wind. In a tizzy of elevation

they reel against the frozen pane
where, inside, in falling light,
the roman candle of the kaffir lily
has flowered at last, has leapt

giddily onto the gray proscenium—
a jongleur tossing bright bells!
a fire eater rising from a circle of ohs!
a green clown in an orange wig.

After the Storm

Upstream, more noise, new rapids — the creek
constricted by debris, old mud and roots
and fallen trees — another sandbar since the storm.

That dead maple fell last spring, made pockets
of dead water, a foulness nothing could clear out.
Now the storm has lanced them, scoured them clean.

A young spruce springs from underneath, rooted
in the other bank, growing hard for the light.
Tiny cones like Christmas decorations.

The sycamores are glowing white as birch.
Tiger lilies blaze from billows of faded goldenrod.
Milkweed boats release their last bright silks.

All of us carried in this current— storm and drought,
failures and redemptions, old mud and sour roots,
caught in these hard rapids, scouring clear.

All Saints Eve

At dawn
leaf-ammil flashes
morse for sun.

Old texts of tires
melt
into highway margins.

Syllables of maple
branches lose
their thousand tongues.

Leaves molder
into veins, ghost hands
signing: fire.

November by Cazenovia Creek

Clear sky, flying clouds. Elsewhere
a terrible storm, tornados
in the southeast, hail
in the Dakotas, in Buffalo,
high winds. But here along the creek,
in thin late-afternoon sun,
in Arleen's woods,

only the sound of the river,
wind held in the cupped
hands of trees.
Molasses sunlight, a tang
of darkness. The afternoon
distilling. Over the creek,
one last dragonfly.

Leaf by leaf, stem by stem, wing
by wing, light releases
the thing it holds. Releases
the cups of my lifted hands—
spotted, knot-boned, odd
as an old branch. Thumb joints
like dragonflies.

A few late berries, a few asters,
and this bush with the light
behind it: nests of whitish fluff,
fibrous, coherent—
within each, a single dark seed.

First Snow

Snow falling though moonlight,
slow as mothwings. Now, ink-
blotch clouds pour in squadrons
over the bare black tops of trees.

Sumi-e trees, night wash
caught in their fanned-out
fingers and branchy hair.
The sky wheels overhead.

Along the road, children
huddle in sheds, in darkness,
watching for the school bus,
yellow as a sun.

WINTER SOLSTICE

Snow fills the downstairs windows,
the soft green hands of pines,
the blurred angel of my winged body.

Beyond the house are broken maples,
ice-choked creek. Swords glitter
from the gutters. All day

the furnace labors. We light candles,
wrap ourselves in blankets,
sleep beside the fire

We wake in darkness, watching.
A spark, then flame—
roses bloom in every icy pane.

Winter in Buffalo

We who abandon you
after the solstice, the white
Christmas, the fool's
bells and new year's
revelations

forget how it settles in,
breath pinned to the throat
by shards of wind, ice
creeping toward the skull-line,
toward the heart

(and the campfires
of music and poetry,
throwing open the door
to the bright cave,
arms full of food and books).

We who do not see it through
can never look eye
to eye and recognize
that landscape
behind the socket:

that landscape of gray
ice, gray
sky, gray
coming under
the door

(the exhalation
going on longer
than anyone can bear.
The scraped bottom
of faith).

By April it has become
something else:
the moment
before the head
crowns.

The sliver of ice
withdraws.
It is over.
And we are home.
But we are never kin.

Acknowledgments

"Fat Time" won the New Millennium Writings Poetry Award and was published in *New Millennium Writings* in Fall 2007.

Here Along Cazenovia Creek was choreographed and performed as "Dancing the Seasons" by Shizuno Nasu in 2012.

About Ruth Thompson

Ruth Thompson's "fierce, gorgeous, sensual" poems of earth-as-body and body-as-earth have been collected in three books of poetry: *Crazing*, *Woman With Crows*, and *Here Along Cazenovia Creek*.

Her award-winning poems appear in *Tupelo Quarterly*, *Sow's Ear Poetry Review*, *New Millennium Writings*, *Chautauqua*, *Potomac Review*, *Naugatuck River Review*, and elsewhere. They have been choreographed by dancers Shizuno Nasu and Jennifer Eng.

Ruth received a BA from Stanford and a doctorate in English from Indiana University. She now lives in Hilo, Hawai'i where she teaches writing, meditation, and yoga.

Recently Ruth has been exploring video and other ways to recreate the unique, sometimes transformative experience — both for her and for the audience — of speaking her poems aloud.

Several videos (including of Ruth discussing her work, of dance performances, and "video poetry") are available at www.ruththompson.net.

www.ingramcontent.com/pod-product-compliance
Lightning Source LLC
Chambersburg PA
CBHW022023290426
44109CB00015B/1286